Water, Tongues, Earth, and Blood

poems by

Charles Darnell

Finishing Line Press
Georgetown, Kentucky

Water, Tongues, Earth, and Blood

*Dedicated to The Sun Poet's Society
for their constant encouragement and enthusiastic support,
especially Rod Carlos Rodriguez, founder and poet.*

Copyright © 2018 by Charles Darnell
ISBN 978-1-63534-400-4 First Edition
All rights reserved under International and Pan-American Copyright Conventions. No part of this book may be reproduced in any manner whatsoever without written permission from the publisher, except in the case of brief quotations embodied in critical articles and reviews.

ACKNOWLEDGMENTS

"My Mother Did Not Read to Me" appeared in *Voices Along the River*, 2011
"Cajun Dreams" appeared in *Voices Along the River*, 2009
"Bayou" appeared in *La Noria*, 2012
"Picking Okra" appeared in *The Luxembourg Review* Autumn, 2016

Publisher: Leah Maines
Editor: Christen Kincaid
Cover Art: Julie Leake
Author Photo: Barbara Darnell
Cover Design: Elizabeth Maines McCleavy

Printed in the USA on acid-free paper.
Order online: www.finishinglinepress.com
also available on amazon.com

Author inquiries and mail orders:
Finishing Line Press
P. O. Box 1626
Georgetown, Kentucky 40324
U. S. A.

Table of Contents

Water, Tongues, Earth and Blood 1

Henderson Swamp 3

Loup Garou 5

Lake Martin 6

Mentor 7

The Last Living Boy from St Martinville 9

Rosary 10

What We Are Named 12

My Mother Did Not Read To Me 13

Green Stalks 14

Bayou 15

Small Town Lonely 17

Picking Okra 19

Crude 21

Cajun Dreams 24

The Bridge Tender 25

Louisiana Harvest 26

Leaving Home 29

Bayou Teche 30

City of the Dead, South Louisiana 31

Raising Cane 32

Water, Tongues, Earth, and Blood

The water moves reluctantly,
unwilling to hurry past
the lush banks
mixed with the wild and
the cultivated.
Lawns run down the slope
right to the edge,
while across,
a riot of tangled
cattails and brambles
arch over the bank.

The sliders bask on
half-sunk logs,
their cousins lurk
below,
snapping at their next meal.

Once a ferry plowed
the slow current,
cypress planks touched
this brown, twisting bayou,
a partnership of nature
and nature bent to man's
service.

Today, a steel bridge
runs across,
detached above,
the drivers hardly aware.

It rolls slowly
past the memorial flame,
remembers the Acadian
settlers who forged a new
home from desperate sorrow.

A little further stands
Evangeline's Oak and
her statue sits,
looking toward the water,
her wooden shoes peek
from beneath a long skirt,
still waiting for her Gabriel.

The old days fade,
and French with them.
Hoary ghosts plead
in that beautiful tongue,
but only whispers in a
still wind,
drowned by the bustle of
another busy day.

I was born here,
my blood is drawn
from the earth of this place.
It calls still,

earth to blood.

Henderson Swamp

The moon is full tonight.
The water calm,
still, like a sheet of glass.
Silhouettes of cypress
point solitary fingers.

Island deer
watch a quiet pirogue
glide through stretches,
move toward
great columns,
row upon row,
holding the highway above
on squat shoulders.

Huge trucks clack
a deep rhythm
across the span,
late night cargo
east to west
and back again.
Alligators sleep
on the bank of mossy tufts,
long accustomed to the noise.

White egrets
stand stark on black legs,
moonlight enhanced statues.
possums waddle
through dead leaves
digging for grubs,
a brief intermission
to the bullfrog chorus
as their big eyes watch carefully.

Before long,
the sun will
chase his pale sister
from the sky
and mist will rise
as charismatic hands of praise,
another day dawning
on Henderson Swamp.

Loup Garou

The swamp is cold tonight,
the moon hides behind
slow clouds,
dark enough for
the hunt.

Those children who
defy their parents,
sneak off to mischief,
are my just prey.

They shall disappear
and "lost in the
swamp" will be
the reason.

But in atavistic
memory
the mind's eye will see
the hairy head,
the snapping jaws
and know in the heart
the truth of it.

Lake Martin

Early morning mist
floats like opaque spirits
chasing the breeze
in and out of soggy cypress,
ripple the open water
and curl through
the cattails without
a sound.

If you wait quiet
by the bank,
the frogs settle
and provide their chorus
thinking you are gone.

Birds light in the
branches and keep
a watchful eye
for food and for you.

Bream break the surface
seeking breakfast
and mosquitoes
find theirs
on your skin.

You slap at the nuisance
and the frogs stop in mid croak.
The birds stare and after
a moment fly off indignant.

You are left with the rising mist
and the sun giving chase,
a quiet day beginning
on a piece of the primordial.

Mentor

Yeats stands at the bow
of the pirogue
right foot on the stabilizer
like Leutze's painting of
Washington.
A poleman shoves
the foamy scum
away from boatside.

"This isn't Byzantium."
Not a question.
He steps onto
the squishy bank,
his pantcuffs already wet,
I set down my traps
and offer him a hand.
He shifts a copy of
The Song of the Wandering
Aengus from
right to left
and I pull him
to drier ground.

He searches the sky
as if looking for his Irish
airman,
but sees only
a solitary Great Blue,
s-shaped neck
above sweeping, slow
wings.

"You lost?"
His chin bumps
the stiff collar
of his painfully white

shirt,
shakes his head.
"I must be here for you.
You write, don't you?"
I nod,
sweat drips off the tip
of my nose,
my chin stubble
holds it
like a dam.

He sweats in earnest now,
away from the breeze
on the water,
his wool jacket
so out of place here.
I suggest he strip
to his shirt and
he shimmies out
one shoulder,
then the other,
rolls up his sleeves
and with pitiless eyes,
"Let's get to work."

So,
the egrets circle
with their raucous cries,
as he moves his slow thighs
in the growing dusk,
up to the shack,
at last, to my pen.

The Last Living Boy from St Martinville

This is not my home,
though it was once.
I walk on the side of the road
in dreams of sugar cane
and soggy ditches.
Shoe toes scuffed
black from crawfish chimneys
kicked absently without looking,
my sweat soaked ball cap
drips from the bill.

The John Deeres
give me room,
The discs sharp
and scintillate in the
morning sun.
They go to cut the
green stalks of cane
so sweet, they fill the air
with the smell of syrup.

I move on different roads now
and this is only
a place I was from,
a boy so long ago
as if I died
and moved to another plane,
another life.

Rosary

My mother spent her life
in the kitchen.
We ate in shifts.
The first watched
a little tv
while the second
sat at the table,
but we all drifted
to the den when
it was time.

Dad would pull out
the rosary with the heavy
tarnished crucifix
and thumb through the
wine colored beads,
droning the words we all knew
but only half believed.

He would kneel on one knee
like a player in a huddle,
his head bowed.
I could see the flakes of dandruff
floating on his sparse hair,
the burn holes in his khakis
from the day's welding sparks.
His voice, so lively in conversation,
adopted a monotone,
a chant worthy of any Buddhist monk.

Mom, so exhausted,
would close her eyes,
hands folded beneath her chin,
I often thought she was dozing,
though her lips moved.

David and I were not allowed
to kneel together,
lest we commit the sacrilege
of horsing around,
our sister, between us,
playing the prayer police.

Our oldest brother
was out on the fringes,
moody and odd.
He had the best position for
a quick retreat
with the last amen.

The little ones fidgeted,
leaning back on their
legs as the beads shoved
their way through Dad's
thick fingers.

When it ended,
they would flock
to their mother's skirt,
my brother and I scramble
to our comic books,
and Dad shuffle to the fridge
for another beer.

What We Are Named

We gather names
hung on us
by those passing
through our lives.

A mother cooing
to her newborn
gives the first,
or perhaps the father.

Other names accumulate,
nicknames, petite noms,
monickers, apodos,
T-Paul, Ta Nan,
Papo,
alll given in love
or ridicule.

We leave them behind
progressing through our years,
they die away
yet their ghosts still call
and echo in our heads.

My Mother Did Not Read To Me

When I was a child,
bedtime came without preamble.
We were whisked into our covers,
pecked hurriedly on our cheeks
after hurried prayers,
and the light went out. Snap!

We'd lie in bed, whispering across the room,
listening to footfalls in the hall,
or the clatter of late night dish washing.
No, my mother did not read to me.

I would often think of how it might have looked,
my head propped on plump pillows,
covers up to my chin on cold winter nights.
or perhaps laying on my side
with my head held by hand and crooked elbow
on a warm summer evening,
listening to the sweet drama
of my animated mother,
her figure back-lit by the lamp
like a Norman Rockwell painting.

No, my mother did not read to me,
nor my brothers, nor my sisters.
She told us the stories we needed
with the washing of the clothes,
the cooking of the meals,
the dressing up for school,
and the smiles and kisses
as we rushed out into the world.

Green Stalks

August.
The cane is tall
but droops in its
endless rows,
beaten by remorseless sun.

Rain does wonders
to their stature,
long leaves rise,
point to a heaven
cloudy and sodden.

In October,
the reapers come,
cut these green stalks
as with a razor.

The cane is gathered
by great pincers,
lifted into giant carts
and carried to the
refinery running
day and night.
white smoke bellows from
old brick stacks.

There, they are crushed
for their juice
and shredded for fodder.
The sap boiled
and dried,
the brown grains
the first step
in a journey
to your table.

Bayou

The Teche was formed
by the wallow of a great snake
say the old Indians.
The serpentine meanderings
lend credence to such stories.
It moves slowly,
indeed, you cannot tell
it flows at all
unless you throw
a stick out into the current.

Life here takes its cue
from the unhurried water.
No one moves too fast
and talk is slow.
Cars move as if
in a permanent school zone.
They move reluctantly
with the changing of the stoplight,
crawling up to walking speed
where no one walks if they can sit.

Stories told in French and accented
English are of old times
and gossip tends toward
who has died lately.
They talk of what year of sugarcane
the Hebert's are in
who's off shore this week,
and everyone holds on
"til Saturday night and
the Fait Do-Do.

No matter how sleepless
or how much the head hurts
they trudge to Mass
on Sunday, the real end times
of the week.
The afternoon spent in a
return to the slow rhythm
and aimless wandering
of another day on the banks
of the bayou.

Small Town Lonely

I
She dries the last cup
along with her tears,
doesn't answer when
asked, "What's wrong, Mommy?"

She puts it with
the ones he used to use,
too many now.

She bends down,
kisses her good night,
makes a smile
to reassure.

II
He sweeps the floor
though it was clean
an hour ago.
The last customer gone
before then.
Night comes early here.

He locks up,
turns the key back and
locks it again,
double check out of habit.
A sigh and a turn for home,
no one waiting for him.

III
She sits in her rocker on the porch,
watching infrequent cars.
The sun sinks
and her old bones crack
as she rises,
Skip supper tonight
she thinks.

Not much to do
since he passed,
cooking for one is lonesome.
She puts on her gown
though there's daylight
and still, lays on her half of the bed.

IV
He scratches some words
on a legal pad,
struggles to find inspiration.
sermons are getting repetitious.
He looks at the Crucified Christ
hung on the wall above
but no help,
despite a mumbled prayer.

God has turned in for the night,
It comes early here.
being alone comes early here.

He thinks of his congregation
and the Beatles,
"All the lonely people,
where do they all come from?
All the lonely people,
where do they all belong?"

They belong here
in this small town.

Picking Okra

This garden has grown
Many years here,
Tomatoes, peppers, squash,
All had their time.
Oh, we still grow them,
But this year we tried okra.

Fall seems best for us,
The blazing heat of summer
Fades, the days are
Still long enough,
Though they shorten.

The okra grows
Waist high,
And we learned
To pinch the tops
So they branch out.
What we didn't know
Was about the pods.

They grow
In their pale greenness
Straight up,
Pushing the dead
Petals of the okra flower
Ahead with the tip,
And they grow fast,
A pod too small in the morning,
May be too big by sundown,
Not good for steaming
Or for the fry pan,
Maybe good still for gumbo.

Each vegetable we plant
Has its own ways,
Its own season,
Much like us,
And we learn to adjust,
Go with the flow,
As they say,
Not a bad life's lesson,
In the garden.

Crude

She waits.
The sticky evening,
smothering and close,
her sweat clings to her upper lip,
the kids too hot to cut up.
The cooler squeaks
its eternal cycle,
but no cool comes.

The sun sinks low
as his truck pulls in,
windows rolled down,
his forearm burnt
from too long on
the road.

He is bone tired,
his smile doesn't reach
his eyes.

He shuffles to the screen door,
pecks her on the lips,
pushed back by the tackle
of kids,
Daddy's home.

He smells of oil and sweat.
she says nothing,
serves him a beer,
cooks up the rice and gravy
and the kids turn up
their noses.
Too bad,
they had their choice all
week.

They eat in silence,
the kids picking at it
with frowns and elbows
until she asks,
"How was the shift?"
He sighs a sorrow
And says,
"Sam was med-evaced
Thursday. Lost some fingers.
On his right hand too."

She winces,
could've been him.

She waits,
listening to the shower hiss,
water washing the easy grime
but not the deep down dirt.
He towels off,
she knows there will be
no second use without a
bleaching.

His rough hands gentle
on her skin,
she smiles at his caresses,
kisses his neck,
the odor of oil distant now,
but insistent.
She strokes the water drops
left between his shoulder blades
as he holds her close.

She waits,
while his hands grow restless,
pulling at her gown,
she wraps her legs
'round his hips
gives him what he needs,
holds him after
and they rock,
he dreams of
the waves that undulate
beneath the crew boat,
taking him to the platform,
the sound of sea gulls
and smell of sour crude,
rough talk from hard men,
doing hard work,
knowing
she waits.

Cajun Dreams

I doze now on this bench swing on this high porch
while the slow waters of the bayou the Indians called the Teche
flow through and down to the Gulf.
Its cadence was the same when my fathers
were welcomed by the Spanish.
The English burned our farms and drove us out of far Acadia.
The Spanish feared them too, coming west, spreading
like a shadow when the sun sets.
We joined Galvez to help the new Americans
drive them far to the north
and away from this, our new land.

We made our homes here,
raised our children and our cattle,
went to Mass here and built our towns.

Our French is still our own
but only the old people speak it now.
They speak it for the tourists on the square
or in front of St Martin of Tours
or at Evangeline's Oak,
but that is just for show.
Some day the last French words will be spoken
over some café au lait
and crepes with powdered sugar.
The last waltz will be sung at the last Fait Do-Do
on some Saturday night.
But I, when I dream,
I will dream in French.

The Bridge Tender

A ghost now,
the water rolls beneath
as it ever has,
slow,
slipping along the steep
wet,dirty banks,
endless,
winding.
The booth empty
for years,
the windows
no longer see.

The metal grate,
Lazarus unrisen,
no one watches,
no one tends.

There is no boat
sliding up the bayou,
no fisherman
raises his string
of catfish
to a tender smile
no longer there,
not there to halt
the carts,
the cars,
no bars across the road.

Dragonflies set
concentric circles
on their journey,
rippling on
the sluggish water,
no watchman to see.

Louisiana Harvest

Early October.
Summer no longer
sticks to her,
the trickle of sweat
has dried in the channels
along her spine,
but she knows
hard work is ahead.

Her man is
out since before light,
his slow rise to sitting
tells her the years
drag on him too.

She no longer goes
with him to the fields
as she did when younger.
She remembers cutting the cane
where the tractor
could not reach,
sweat pouring off her neck
rolling down between her breasts,
her man smiling,
"Wet t-shirt contest?" he laughs.

She smiles to herself,
remembering there was love after,
there was always time for that,
no matter the tired bones.

Now, Sunday mornings,
maybe.

He goes out with the hired boys,
their own son gone to the city,
a desk man with a city house,
wife, kids, and mortgage.
too soft now,
even if he were willing.

This is the last of it.
He's getting too old
even with the winter's rest.
Too soon, it will start again,
the plowing, replant,
and aches.

It beats a body down,
the Fait- dodo
long forgotten.
Sleep a luxury and
all the entertainment wanted.

She thinks they are dried up,
like the cut cane
left in the field too long.
The juice crystal and hard,
no strength left
for gathering.

She wonders what will become of it,
the cane fields glistening
in the morning damp.
Will a younger family
step up?
She thinks not.
It is passé, old fashioned.
The dirt does not flow
in modern veins.

The cane will grow,
but tended by some
corporate man.
He will see the planting
of dollars,
impatient for the harvest,
a means to profit,
not to nurture the soul.

Leaving Home

Two hours west is suddenly Texas,
follow I-10 mostly.
But before all that,
the Bayou Teche and sugar cane
stretch along LA 31 through Parks
and the old drawbridge at Pont de Breaux.

As you draw toward the interstate,
speed picks up,
like horses sensing a race.
Even the eighteen-wheelers
shift through their gears
with alacrity.

You already miss the slower pace,
time to look out the window
as you roll beneath oaks
dripping Spanish moss.
The cane growing
like green explosions.

But now, you turn on the access road
toward the ramp,
picking up speed
for the run back,
a long way to San Antonio.

I would say I was heading home,
but I put that behind me.

Bayou Teche

I am the brown slow water of rain collected.
I am the snapper sunning on the bank,
the night heron standing still on one leg.

I see the sugarcane greening in the fields,
smell the smoke of those fields burning.
I scrape the earth from the sticky bottom
and carry Acadiana to the sea.

City of the Dead, South Louisiana

There's no six feet under
there, the water table
too high.
All the dead are resting
above ground,
laid out in brick tombs
plastered over,
names and dates chiseled
to fade with time.
No dead swim in mud
slurries
visiting their neighbors
up the row
or day trips to another
boneyard down the highway.

They lay still on stone pallets,
cramped and cold,
crying angels guard the corners
of their tombs.

Raising Cane

Early October
and the sugar mill
at St. John's
is crowned
by white smoke,
like the Vatican
announcing a
new Pope.

The line of great carts
wait to unburden
themselves
and return to
the field to be
loaded down
with another
green mound.

But before all that,
he walks on the
muddy black earth,
carries an armload
of stripped stalks,
he selected,
looks down the length,
like checking lumber
for warping,
makes sure the joints
are evenly spaced.

He moves along
the raised beds,
lays the green,
sticky rods
as if laying pipe.

He goes the whole
length,
stands up to see
his son staring back.
"There's machines for that,"
he says.
"I know"
and bends down to cover
what he laid
with bare hands.
He knows
his boy is shaking his head.

He does it for his soul,
the connection of life
to the earth
from which he came
and will return soon enough.
The black dirt sticks
to his fingers,
packs under his nails,
and he pats the rows
down to a rhythm
he learned from the
memory of his father's
father.

Charles Darnell was born in St Martinville, LA and lived in the area for only a short time before his parents and siblings moved to east Texas. His father moved progressively further west as the family grew in search of the blue collar jobs he did to support an eventual brood of nine children. He spent most of his career working near San Antonio, TX.

Charles grew up in and around the San Antonio area, but spent summer days with cousins and aunts and uncles in cajun country. His parents, James and Mary Darnell, brought their cajun culture, food, religion, language, and work ethic to Texas and instilled these values in their children.

Charles graduated from The University of Texas at Austin and married a San Antonio girl, Barbara Pierce, to whom he has been married for 45 years. They have two children and two grandchildren.

Charles began writing poetry casually. He wrote a few poems in college after encouragement by one of his English Literature professors, but did not begin to take his writing seriously until he was nearly 60.

On a whim, he entered a few poems in a local poetry fair and received some modest recognition. He eventually won The San Antonio Poetry Fair Award in 2010 and the Tempie Skerritt-Hickman Award that same year. In 2013, Charles' poem "Waiting for Joy" won the *On Fire* poetry contest in Bangalore, India.

In 2012, Charles began attending the Sun Poets Society open-mic sessions and began submitting poems to anthologies, literary and popular magazines, journals, and online websites. He has had dozens of individual poems published in such journals as *The Enigmatist, Ocotillo Review, Texas Observer, Still Crazy,* and *Harbinger Asylum*. His poetry blog, *Speaking*

In Colors, has received over 30,000 page views since its launch in May, 2012. Charles manages an online poetry critque group, The Poetry Construction Site, an international group of poets providing supportive critque to its members.

Charles continues to attend the weekly open-mic sessions with the Sun Poets and can be found reading and listening to other poets every Wednesday night.

www.ingramcontent.com/pod-product-compliance
Lightning Source LLC
LaVergne TN
LVHW041559070426
835507LV00011B/1176